Author - Natalie Shutlar
Editor - Annette Hobday

IT'S OK TO WORRY

A children's book about anxiety and how to deal with it

By
Natalie Shutlar

For Caleb and Gracie, my sunshine even on the cloudiest of days.

This is Gracie; she's 7 years old.

She is brave
and
beautiful;
strong and
bold.

Sometimes Gracie feels worried and sad.

But she doesn't want to make the grown-ups feel bad.

It's
hard
at times
to know
what to do.

Not knowing who
to turn to; who will
listen to you.

So, it's important to talk

to someone you trust.

To help
you
feel brighter,
this is
a must.

Sharing your problems will make you feel better.

If you don't want to talk, try writing a letter.

Gracie has learned

that it's better to talk...

...to take a
deep breath
or
go for
a walk.

When Gracie is scared or lonely or sad...

...she speaks to
her brother,

her Mum,
or her Dad.

Grown-ups have worries all of their own...

...but they share when they're scared so they don't feel alone.

We all worry sometimes, and that's OK!

Is there anything that's on your mind today?

....

....

....

....

....

....

Printed in Great Britain
by Amazon